The Upside Down House

and Other Poems

Written and Illustrated by

Debbie and Jennifer Sleeper

FCP

Full Court Press
Englewood Cliffs, New Jersey

First Edition

Copyright © 2011 by Debbie Sleeper and Jennifer Sleeper

Published in the United States of America
by Full Court Press, 601 Palisade Avenue
Englewood Cliffs, NJ 07632

ISBN 978-0-9833711-3-7
Library of Congress Control No. 2011927086

Book Design and Editing by Barry Sheinkopf for Bookshapers
(www.bookshapers.com)
Colophon by Liz Sedlack

To our loving parents, Ann and Bob, who raised us to appreciate the power of laughter and the pleasure of words.

Special thanks to you and to all our friends for your valued opinions and support.

TABLE OF CONTENTS

ADVENTURES

Yesterday I was a knight who fought an epic battle.
Today I was a cowboy riding horses with no saddle.
Tomorrow I'll hunt aliens and maybe catch a crook—
I never know what to expect when opening a book.

THE UPSIDE DOWN HOUSE

Welcome my friends, to the Upside Down House!
It's only ten dollars a tour!
And all of your children, your friends and your spouse
are bound to enjoy it, I'm sure!

First we enter through the attic window.
It's dusty, so try not to sneeze.
We'll cross the main rafter with caution and after
that through a trapdoor we will squeeze!

Next we will climb a small ladder
to the bedrooms and bathroom above.
You may find it appealing to nap on the ceiling
or bathe in our Upside Down tub!

Then we will climb the main staircase,
which spirals up to the front hall.
In the kitchen we'll break for some Upside Down cake
from the fridge that is up on the wall!

Come into the Upside Down playroom.
We have games and we have DVDs.
If you climb in a chair and you hold up your hair
you can watch any movie you please!

Now we're done with our tour of the Upside Down House.
You can leave through the door in the hall.
And I'm perfectly sure that you'll come back for more. . .
If you live through the three-story fall!

SHHHH!

We're playing a game of hide and seek.
I know I am going to win,
'cause sometime last year little Johnny hid here,
and nobody ever found him!

MOOSE ON THE LOOSE!

There's a moose on the loose in the hallway,
and nobody knows what to do.
We're really not sure where he came from.
He must have escaped from the zoo.

He's trampled through all of our classrooms,
destroying the tables and desks.
He's chewed all our pens and erasers,
and eaten our papers and tests.

I just tried to go to the bathroom
to rinse off my hands at the sink,
when he came running in here and squished me
so he could get by for a drink.

All the teachers have gotten together
and are trying to lasso him down,
but he's jumping right over the lasso
and knocking them all to the ground.

Now the principal's here from his office,
looking frantic and very upset.
He's cornered the moose by the stairwell!
He's tying him up with a net!

Yes, they've captured the moose in the hallway.
We all thought their chances were slim.
Which is why I'm not sure how to tell them
'bout the rhino I saw in the gym!

CLOTHES

My shoes and socks are fighting
'cause my shoe said something rude.
My sock told him to bite his tongue
and drop his attitude.
My shoe said socks were all washed up,
and now my socks refuse
to go within ten paces
of my disrespectful shoes.

My pants and shirt are arguing
because it seems my shirt
found out my pants were flirting
with my blue and yellow skirt.
Now my shirt is torn in sorrow,
and she says there's not a chance
she is ever gonna mend things
with my double-crossing pants.

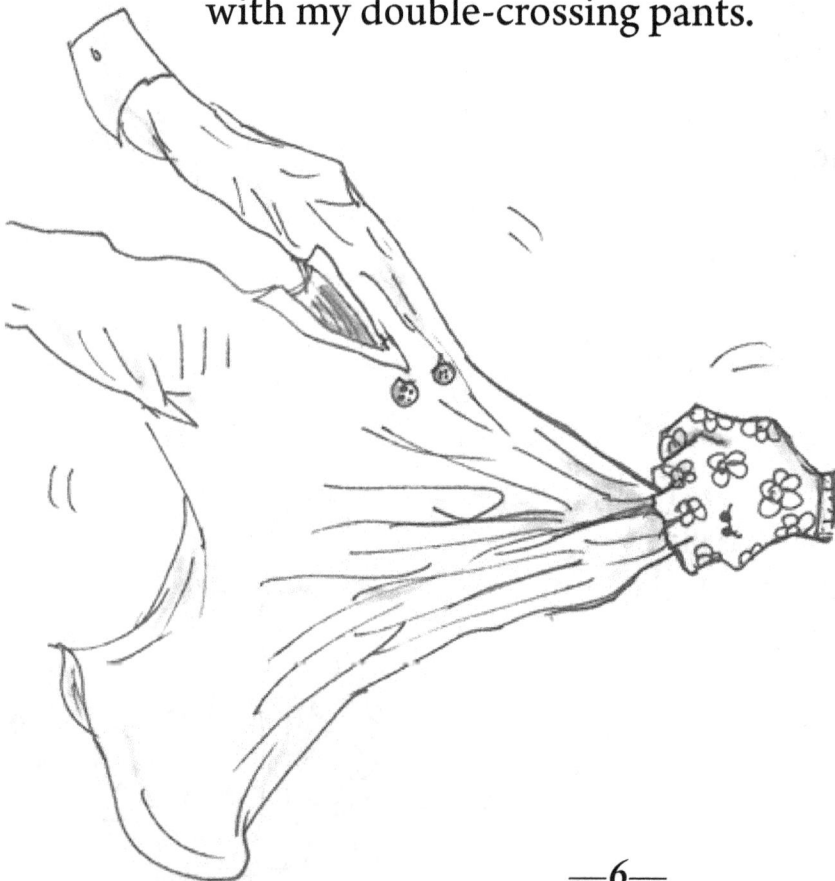

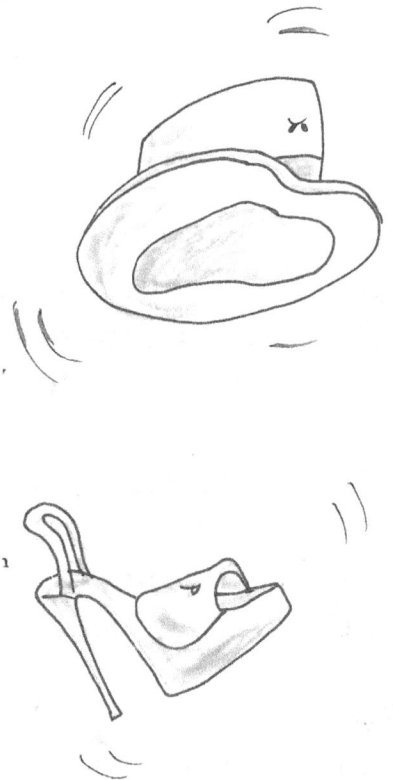

My hat and gloves are quarrelling
about who is the best.
My hat claims he's the greatest
and a head above the rest.
My gloves claim they're more handy
'cause my hat is too uptight,
and now they both refuse to go
within each other's sight.

My clothes are all in arguments.
My coat's a screaming wreck.
My shorts have said my scarf's a pain
in everybody's neck.
My underwear is sobbing
in the corner by the door.
My boots just kicked my flip-flops.
My whole closet is at war!
I don't know how to stop them.
It's a battle zone in there.
Until they stop their fighting
there is nothing I can wear!
I cannot put my clothes on
when they're filled with so much hate.
Guess I'll have to go out naked
'till they all cooperate!

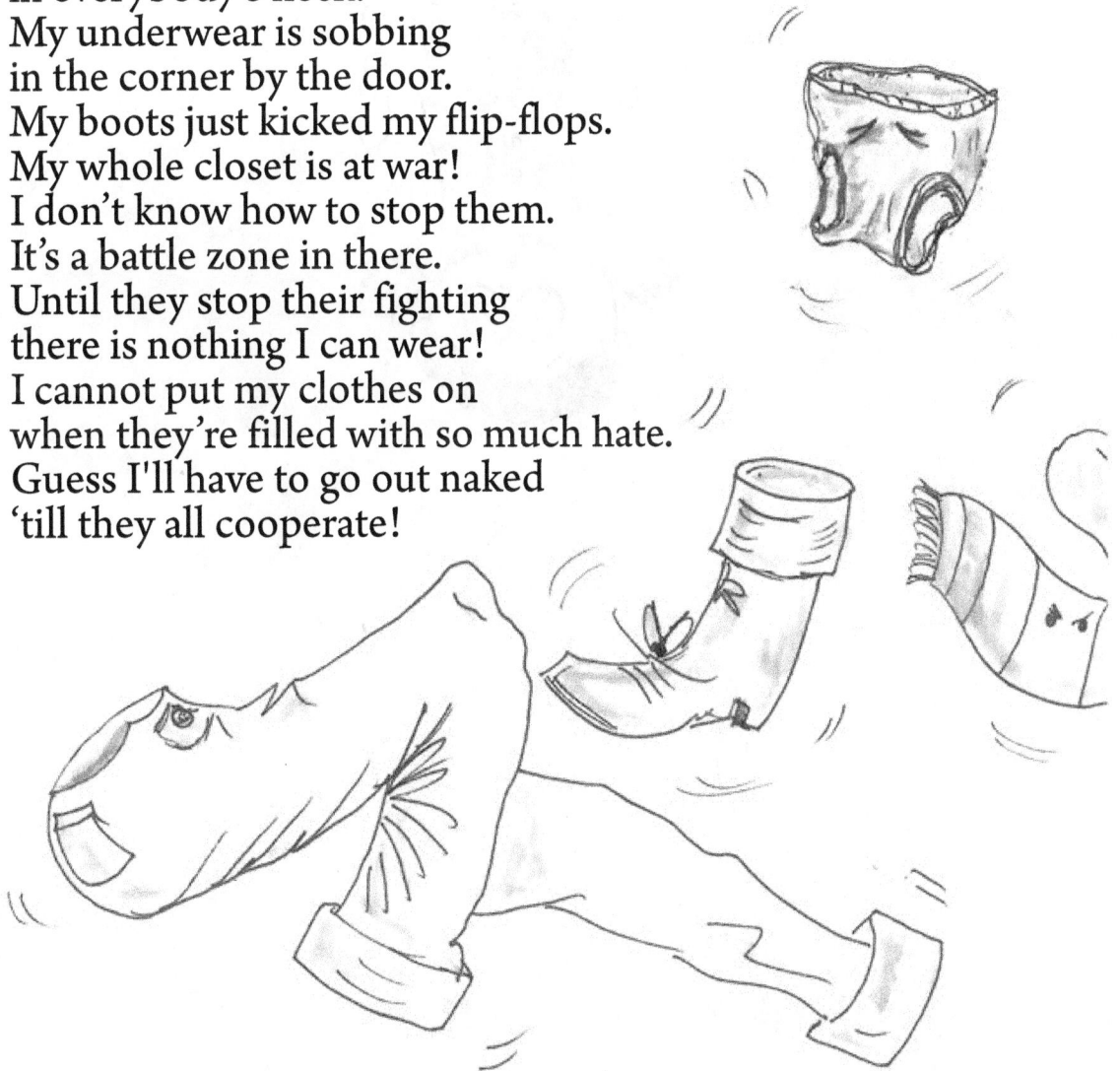

GROWTH STRATEGY

You want to be taller? Here's what you must do:
Cover your ceiling with hot sticky glue.
Now stick your feet to it - make sure they're stuck tight.
Then hang upside down from your ceiling all night.
By day you'll have grown 'bout a foot and a half.
(If not, then at least I'll have had a good laugh!)

NEW CAR

Come hop in my car and I'll drive us both far—
to Ohio, New York or Nebraska.
And if you are lucky, we'll stop in Kentucky,
or ride all the way to Alaska.

From Louisiana or up to Montana,
there's nowhere that we cannot go.
We can even drive straight down to Florida state,
or head out to New Mexico.

So come ride with me in my shiny new car,
this glorious, great hunk of metal.
'Cause I'm sure we can get any place you can bet. . .
just as soon as my feet reach the pedal!

SANTA CLAUS WANTED

We're looking for someone to be Santa Claus
'cause poor Santa Claus broke his hip.
If hired you'll work day and night without pause
for a dollar a day with no tip.

From April till Christmas you'll have to build toys,
though you won't get a gift for yourself.
You'll check twice a list of all good girls and boys
while you supervise every last elf.

You can't go to sleep till the reindeer are fed.
They eat only carrots and wheat.
You alone must assemble the rickety sled
which can break down at ten thousand feet.

You must live way up North, where it's windy and cold,
matching children with gifts they desire.
You must squeeze down the chimney of every household
and hope you don't land in the fire.

We just need one person, one person—just one
to take St. Nick's job for a year.
Won't anyone give up their own Christmas fun
to bring everyone else Christmas cheer?

It's a great job—I promise there is nothing to it!
You'll like living at the North Pole!
Oh, no. . .now the boss says that I'll have to do it!
I'm giving you all lumps of coal!

BAT

Hit a ball with a bat, it's called "baseball," they say,
so I'm going to give it a try.
But how can I smack this here ball with this bat
when the bat keeps on trying to fly?

GIFT

My Dad said he'd get me a gift.
He's always into giving.
I said I would like anything
as long as it was living.

I would not mind a dog or cat,
a parrot or canary.
I won't reject a big insect
or spider fat and hairy.

I'd love a sheep or llama
from New Zealand or Peru,
or maybe an iguana,
or a baby kangaroo.

An elephant's amazing
and a penguin's worth a laugh.
Our backyard's good for grazing
with a zebra or giraffe.

Now Dad says my new gift's outside,
though small, due to his budget.
He says that I can feed it
but it may hurt when I touch it.

No problem, I'm still happy
that a living pet is mine!
I just know it's a dingo
or a little porcupine!

I hope I find it fast or I'll
be late for soccer practice…
I'm sure that I will see it once
I move this stupid cactus!

SOMETHING STINKY

There's something stinky in the fridge I can't identify.
It could be last week's spinach soup or Thursday's cabbage pie.
It could be all that liverwurst I bought last month on sale.
It may be year-old chunky cheese or moldy bread gone stale.
I cannot say what it could be from just the sight and smell....
Why don't you take a bite for me and see if you can tell?

GEOGRAPHY

I just failed my geography test!
I wish my teacher curved it …
I just failed my geography test!
I don't think I deserved it!

'Cause we all know that Canada borders Kuwait,
that England's in France and that China's a state.
So I can't blame anything else but Fate
that I failed my geography test!

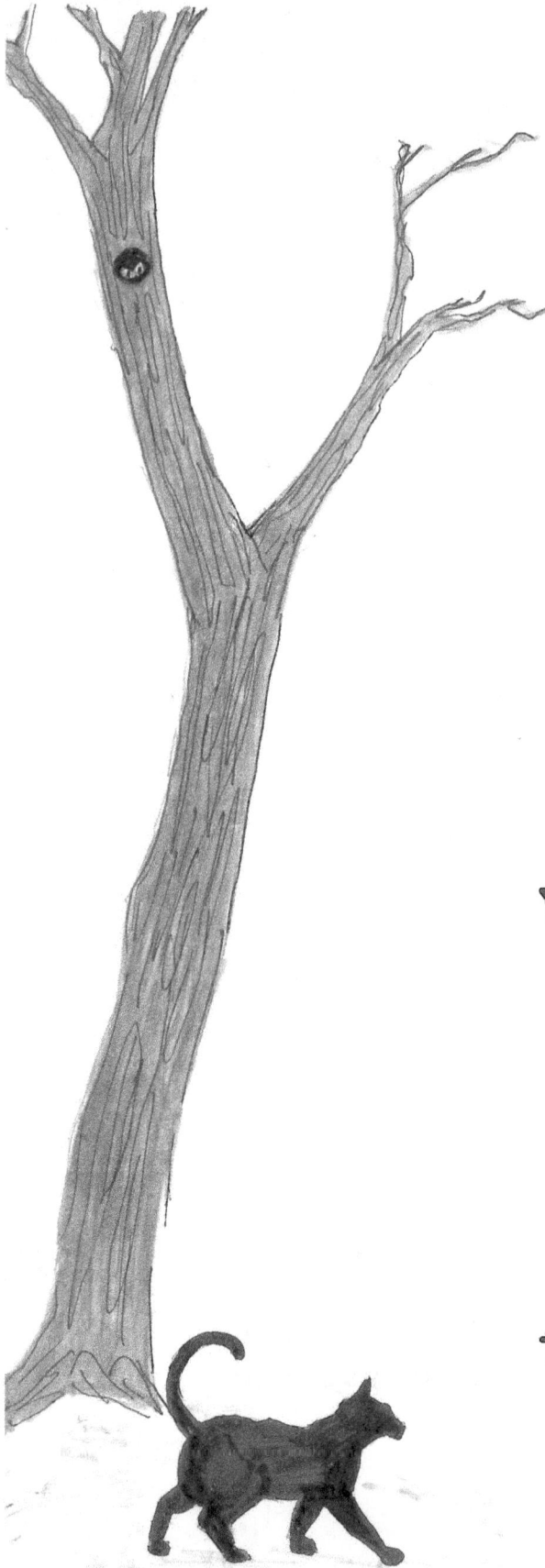

The Thirteenth Poem

Welcome to the thirteenth poem

right here inside this book you own.

For everyone who's read this verse

has suffered some unlucky curse...

You're reading it? That means you're next!

Stop, or else you will get hexed!

Close this book right now—just do it!

Fold this page in half and glue it!

There's still some time to change your fate!

Too late.

HELPFUL

Look, Mom, I finished all my chores:
I washed the windows and the floors.
I did my homework, mowed the grass,
I tidied up my room at last.
I did the laundry and the dishes.
Let me give you fifteen kisses!
I love you very much, you know. . .
So how did Back-to-School Night go?

SOLID STOMACH STEVEN

Solid Stomach Steven,
who is only ten years old,
has eaten every meal
our cafeteria has sold.

And Steven seems to like the food
and finds it quite a treat.
So every afternoon we gather
round to watch him eat.

On Monday we had deep-fried filth
with monkey soup and gore.
And Susie Snite tried just one bite
and passed out on the floor.

But Solid Stomach Steven grinned
and ate the whole huge pile.
"My compliments go to the chef,"
he told us with a smile.

On Tuesday they served lizard toes
and garnished warthog snout.
And Tommy Tiff just took a whiff
and blew his nostrils out.

But Solid Stomach Steven
ate the toes, the nose and all.
"That was a most delicious feast,"
we heard ol' Steven call.

On Wednesday we had walrus
with a side dish of dead flies.
And Sarah Smith just looked at it
and out popped both her eyes.

But Steven ate the whole thing up
and all the flies as well.
"My gosh, that meal! It was unreal!"
we heard old Steven yell.

On Thursday we had meatloaf.
It was harder than a rock.
And Joe just thought about it
and fell over from the shock.

But Steven swallowed everything
in just a gulp or two.
He didn't chip a single tooth—
he didn't even chew!

Oh, how did Steven do it?
Was his stomach made of steel?
It really did amaze us
how he wolfed down every meal.

He'd grab and slurp and gulp and burp,
and always clean his plate.
I don't think even Superman
could eat what Steven ate!

On Friday we had pizza,
every student's favorite treat.
And probably the only meal
that we would ever eat.

But Solid Stomach Steven
eyed the pizza with a moan.
"Oh, yuck," he said, "I'm glad today
I brought my lunch from home."

ACCIDENT PRONE

I'm accident-prone, yes, accident-prone—
the biggest klutz you've ever known!

I've slipped on rugs and tripped on chairs,
I've tumbled down twelve flights of stairs.
I promise you I cannot swim,
but see that lake? I've fallen in!
I've stapled paper to my thigh,
and put my finger in my eye.
I've spilled the milk and stained the rug,
broke the window, pulled the plug,
I've choked on cookies and on cakes
and stepped on twenty different rakes.
Dad's relieved that I don't drive.
(Mom's surprised I'm still alive.)

Yes, I'm a klutz, but still I swear,
I've NEVER needed doctor's care!
And now before it gets too late,
I think I'll go outside and skate.
Oh, gee! Oh, whee! Hey, this is fun!
Crash! Ouch! Help! Call 911!

THE HOG ATE MY HOMEWORK

The hog ate my homework, he ate all the homework
I worked on for hours last night.
My history homework! My chemistry homework!
He swallowed it down in one bite.

The hog ate my homework, he ate all my homework,
but maybe I'll still get my "A"s
if I go get a sack and I sit by his back,
and I wait for a couple of days.

LEPRECHAUN HUNT

This morning, while I was out mowing my lawn,
I happened to spot me an ol' leprechaun
right down by the bushes. He blended in slightly,
until I saw little green eyes glinting brightly.
I grabbed the old net that I use when I fish
and ran out to grab him and get me a wish!
But he slipped from my grip and ran into the dawn,
so I'm fast on the heels of that ol' leprechaun!

He sings, "Hi tiddly-aye tiddly-my tiddly tee.
Keep running lad, 'cause you'll never catch me!"

I've followed this leprechaun two days or more.
We've crossed the whole country and reached a dark shore.
And one time I caught his right sleeve in my fist,
but he slipped off his coat and ran into the mist!
And now I can see a bright rainbow up there.
He seems to be climbing it up through the air!
That's not gonna' stop me! I'm jumping right on,
'cause I'm going to catch me that ol' leprechaun!

He sings, "Lo tiddly-oh tiddly-mo tiddly tee.
Keep climbing lad, 'cause you'll never catch me!"

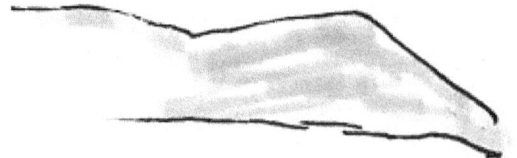

I caught that ol' leprechaun, caught him at last!
I told you I would —even though he ran fast!
He stopped when we came to his world, strange and haunting.
He said he would grant me that wish I've been wanting!
I could wish for riches or maybe straight A's.
I think I deserve it—I've chased him for days!
In fact. . .oh, dear me, I did not pay attention…
How do I get out of this weird new dimension?
What use are good grades or good fortune and luck,
or riches or powers when here I am stuck?

Trapped in this darkness forever alone!
I wish, oh I wish, how I wish I was home!

WORST NURSE

I think that there is nothing worse
than being sent to see our nurse.
When Bobby saw her for a scrape
she wrapped him up in masking tape.
When Billy Bumpkin had a sneeze
she put six stitches in his knees.
When Barbra Ann was feeling rotten,
both her ears got stuffed with cotton.
When Robbie's hiccups wouldn't cease,
she made him drink a bowl of grease.
When Karen had a swollen throat,
she made her kiss a billy goat!
And everyone she's tried to cure
has felt worse than they did before.
So I will never see our nurse.
I don't care if my kidneys burst!
Or if my tongue swells six feet long!
Or if my teeth all grow in wrong!
If I have awful diarrhea—
even then I'll never see 'er!
Never! Wait! What's that you say?
You say we have our test today?
Oh, teacher, oh! My stomach hurts!
Please, can I go and see the nurse?

STRANGE WHISTLE

I've found the strangest whistle
lying here upon the ground.
And though I've tried to blow it twice,
it does not make a sound.

I'll try to blow it just once more
until my cheeks turn red.
But still I just hear nothing,
so I guess the whistle's dead.

It's neat I found a whistle
even though it is defective.
I always like to start my day
with something unexpected.

STORED

I went down to the storage room
to get some school supplies.
The room was dark and dusty,
and I didn't realize

that the door closed automatically,
so I was rather shocked,
when I tried to open it
and found that it was locked.

Now I'm trapped here in the storage room
with cobwebs everywhere.
There's a rat eating my shoelace
and a spider in my hair.

My voice is hoarse from shouting
and I've pounded, kicked and pried.
But nothing I have done has worked
'cause I'm still trapped inside.

I guess some time may pass before
they see I've not returned.
It may take even longer
till they're worried or concerned.

So if somebody out there reads
or listens to this poem...
Please come unlock the storage room
so that I can go home!

ICKY

Happy birthday, Vicki! Your cake is very sticky.
I made it very quick-y and it was a little tricky.
The icing is too thick-y and it looks a little icky.
(I've always said it's really great
that you're not very picky!)

FEET

I wrote this
poem upon
my feet
But now
I'm feelin'
dumb....

They're much
too small
to write
it neat
Next time
I'll try
My
bum!

AN APPLE A DAY

"An apple a day keeps the doctor away,"
so here's what I thought I would try:
I bought sixty apples one day from the store
and baked them all up in a pie.
For breakfast and lunch I ate pie for a month,
and now I can't understand why
I have to go meet with my doctor next week—
should've known that old quote was a lie!

10 WORD POEM

Wait… I can only
use ten words for this?

Baloney!

BEARTHDAY PRESENT

Someone left me a bearskin rug
while I was out at school.
At first I was a little shocked,
but now I think it's cool.

It was my birthday yesterday.
I guess some friend of mine
came by and left it on the floor,
right here for me to find.

And what a lovely rug it is!
The fur's so soft to feel.
The gleaming eyes and glistening teeth
just make it look so real.

I'll bury both my feet in it. . .
my gosh, this rug is warm!
It's just the thing I need to snuggle
up to in this storm.

This rug is so relaxing I can
feel my muscles soften.
I think that I will leave my door
unlocked a lot more often!

TOMORROW

Tomorrow I'll go on a picnic.
Tomorrow I'll go for a hike.
Tomorrow I'll take the dog to the lake
and then ride round the block on my bike.

Tomorrow I'll clean up the basement.
Tomorrow I'll go to the mall.
Tomorrow Dennis and I will play tennis
and then we'll play catch with our ball.

Tomorrow I'll practice piano.
Tomorrow I'll climb up a tree.
Tomorrow I'll swim and I'll go to the gym—
But today I am watching TV.

TEACHER CREATURE

Ever since we got back from our trip to the zoo,
our teacher's been acting quite strange.
What's different about her? We haven't a clue.
It's something we can't quite explain.

She watches us all with her large, beady eyes
from the edge of a recipe book.
She's turned up the heat in the classroom so high
it feels like we're starting to cook.

Her skin seems a little bit scaly and green.
Her nose seems a little too big.
The teeth in her smile have grown 'bout a mile.
I think she is wearing a wig.

She often will walk round the classroom,
but never to check on our spelling.
Instead she will baste us, and often she'll taste us
and tell us how good we are smelling.

And every time I see that look in her eye,
her gaze makes my skin kind of crawl,
and we haven't seen Joe since an hour ago
when she called him out into the hall.

Yes, something is different 'bout teacher.
But we haven't a guess or a hunch.
It's a puzzle. Oh, well! There's the twelve o' clock bell!
Perhaps we'll find out after lunch!

STRING

Hey, look! I found a piece of string.
It really is the strangest thing.
I'm looking all around - by gum!
I can't tell where it's coming from.
I'll give that string a great big tug.
It isn't coming from the rug.
It isn't coming from Mom's dress.
Where does it lead? I cannot guess.
I just keep reeling in this bit.
There seems to be no end to it.
I'll tug until the answer's clear,
but gosh, it's getting cold in here!

BEARDED

Melinda McGreerd is a little bit weird:
Last night she grew a long white beard.
She said with a sigh,
"I can't understand why
all this hair on my chin has appeared."

"I just woke up in bed, and I'd grown one," she said,
looking terribly angry and shaking her head.
"And I don't think it's fair
that my chin sprouted hair
when I wanted a moustache instead."

OH, WON'T SOMEONE PLEASE ASK THE GRUNK TO THE DANCE?

Oh, won't someone please ask the Grunk to the dance?
He'd just like a partner, you see.
I think you will find if you give him a chance
he's as sweet as a monster can be.

With flowers in hand, he'll show up at your door.
Though your instincts may tell you to run,
you'll quickly find out when you hit the dance floor
that the Grunk is incredibly fun!

You can dance every song and he'll never wear out.
Each contest you'll win without fail.
You will jump, stomp, and clap as you boogie about.
(Just be sure to watch out for his tail!)

So please, go ahead, ask the Grunk to the dance.
He'll for sure make your evening a winner…
But after the dance I would not take the chance
of accepting his invite to dinner!

KNOW IT ALL

I know if there's one thing the zoo won't allow,
it's teasing the lion—like you're doing now.
I told you that twice, but unfortunately
I also know you never listen to me.

MAGIC DANCING SHOES

Susie had a lovely pair
of magic dancing shoes.
Because of them there was no
competition she could lose.
And Lucy was unlucky
for she did not have a pair
of magic dancing shoes like those
that Susie got to wear.

So Lucy chose to practice
and the months and years went by,
and soon she was a dancer—
she could jump and leap and fly!
While Susie, on the other hand,
took out her shoes one night,
and found she could not get them on.
Alas, they were too tight.

And at the dancing contest
Lucy danced with grace and style.
She won it by a landslide—
what she'd wanted all the while.
And Susie, with her magic shoes
which then had grown too small,
had never practiced on her own
and could not dance at all.

So here's a lesson to be learned
for when you might compete:
Just practice hard and you will find
the magic in your feet.

SHIPWRECK

Captain:
I'm captain of this ship I love,
but I've just made a blunder.
Would you believe I've hit a reef
and now we're going under?

    First Mate:
    At least the coast is pretty close,
    'cause look, I see a seagull.
    Before we bolt I'll just consult
    the rules, so all is legal.

    I think we're fine. . .wait, never mind!
    I've just looked at this quote:
    "In any bust the captain must
    go down with his own boat."

Captain:
Hey, let me look at that rulebook. . . .
My goodness—it's all true.
The ship goes down, the captain drowns!
Whatever shall I do?

    First Mate:
    A silly rule, unjust and cruel,
    I can't believe it's stated.
    Just find the place where it's erased.
    It has to be outdated.

Captain:
Oh, what's the use—there's no excuse!
I must stay on the boat.
I'll just request a good life vest,
so I can stay afloat.

    First Mate:
    Well, sorry, Captain, that can't happen.
    I recall the reading:
    It says 'go down,' not 'float around.'
    You can't do that, it's cheating.

And now I should be going—
would you mind if I just take
our pets: the fish and Mr. Hiss,
the baby water snake?

Captain:
Okay, farewell. . . I guess I shall
go do something amusing.
Like drink some Port and build a fort
of lifeboats they're not using.

Or maybe look at that rulebook,
which really needs revision.
If I could get away, you bet
I'd write the new edition!

It's pretty clear my end is near!
I'm trying not to panic. . .
Especially 'cause this rulebook was
last used on the Titanic!

CAUGHT

When some folks go fishing
they catch fish galore.
My friend caught six trout,
and my cousin caught more.

But I just went fishing. . . .
Oh, how can this be?
I caught not one fish,
but a big fish caught me.

SWEET DREAMS

Last night after I went to bed,
I had the most wonderful dream.
I dreamt of a land that had sugar for sand
and snow of vanilla ice cream.

The houses were carved out of rich chocolate fudge
with rooftops of mousse freshly made.
There were lollipop flowers, and when there were showers
it rained only pink lemonade.

The sun was a honey drop up in the sky
that melted the coconut dew.
The trees were so dandy—they were cotton candy
in sticks spun in purple and blue!

And all of the sugar, the ice cream and snacks,
the chocolate and every sweet,
from the Mountains of Cake to the Great Pudding Lake,
was made for me to eat!

This morning I woke up and felt strangely full
from that wonderful sugary banquet.
Now I know what it means when they tell you "sweet dreams!"
But where in the world is my blanket?

RUMORS

Lee said that Bill had a big crush on Jill.
Bill said that Nick knew an ex-convict.
Nick said that Jack lived alone in a shack.
Jack said that Lance sometimes still wets his pants.
Lance said that Lee was as dumb as could be. . .
and I hate to think what they all say about me!

MR. MCMILLER

Mr. McMiller, the bloodthirsty killer,
has quite a few names that I know.
He's been called "Stranglin' Phil,"
and "Slice Them Up Bill,"
"The Crusher," and "Cut Your Throat Joe."

And if you should meet him, you may wish to greet him
as "Crazy ol' Fred" or "McStab."
You're welcome to use
any name that you choose,
but I'll stick to calling him Dad!

CROSSING

My folks said I'd get hurt if I don't
look before I cross.
But I think that I can show those silly
cars and trucks who's boss!

Instead of looking left and right
(which always takes so long.)
I'll run straight through the traffic—
Phew! My folks are always wrong!

263187540

Some numbers met 4 lunch today;
they had some tea and cake.
And number 1 brought cookies, 1
4 each of them 2 take.
So 0 he passed 1, 2, 3,
and that left 3 ,4, 5
to save 4, 6, and 7,
who had yet to arrive.
But greedy 5, he took all 3
and munched them all, but luckily
when 6 and 7 walked in late
they said that they already 8.

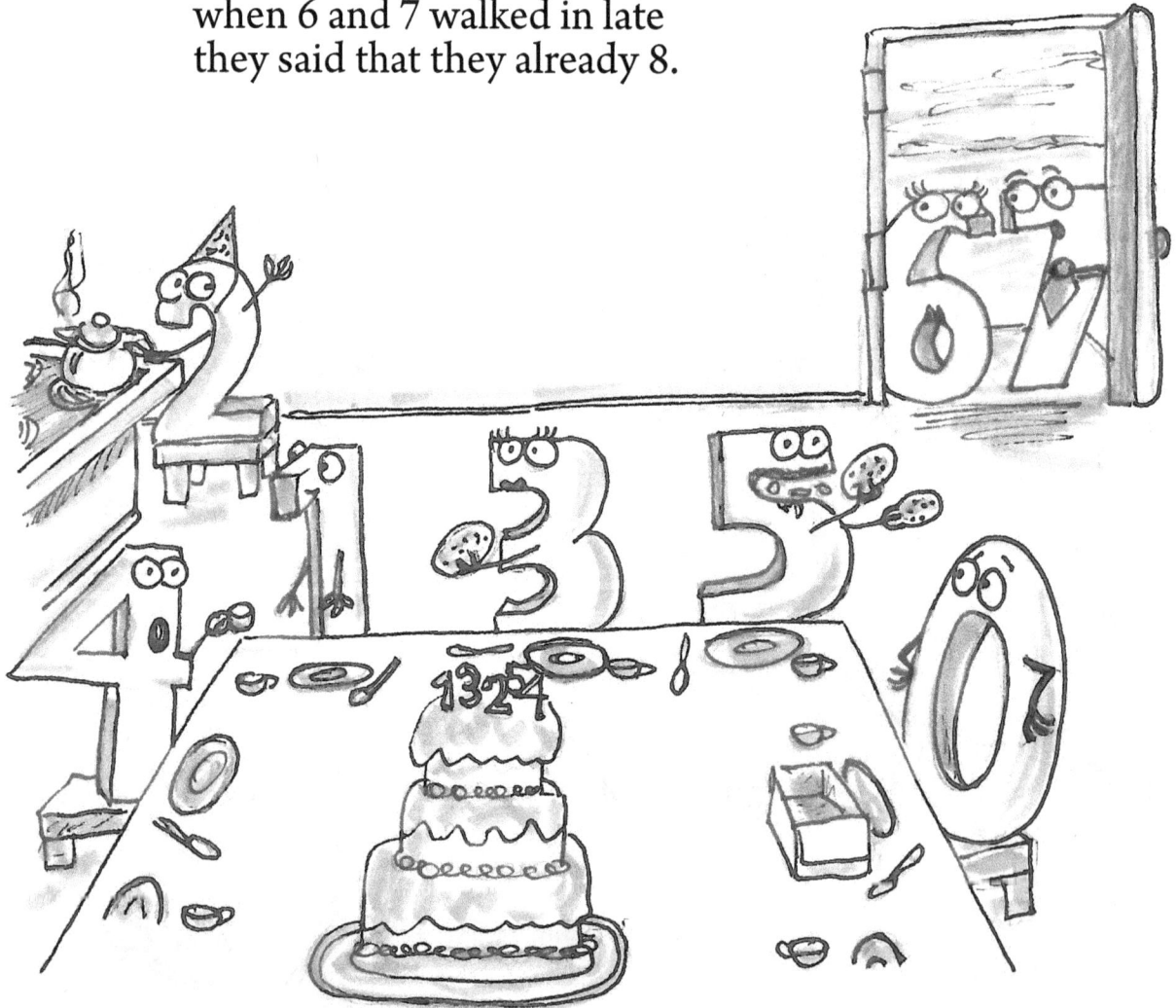

GLASS EYE

Gramps lost his glass eye today.
He says he just can't find it.
Says he looked beneath the bed
and even looked behind it.

"I guess it's gone for good," he says,
and hangs his head in sorrow.
I say, "Let's have some lemonade,
and look for it tomorrow!"

TALENT

Hello, dear sir, my name is Tim
and this is John, my star.
Now if you want to see an act
then just stay where you are!
You say you need some talent,
but it's just too hard to find?
Well, Johnny here's got talent
and an act to blow your mind!

See look, he rides this bicycle.
He peddles with his hands
while juggling some carving knives
then with a flip, he stands,
and eats some red hot peppers
while he walks across a wire.
And then he does a somersault
right through this ring of fire!

And now, watch as he puts his head
between this lion's jaws.
And next he'll lift a red sedan—
but please hold your applause,
'cause John still has to do a trick
upon this trampoline:
like whistlin' some Beethoven
while drinking gasoline!

And now we've reached the final act:
First Johnny does the limbo,
and then he catapults himself
right through your office window!
Wait, what was that? Why, no, my friend,
you never said before
that your talent office here was on
the thirty-seventh floor!
Well, I'm glad you liked our act
and want to put us on. . .
But first I must find someone else
as talented as John!

SCARED

I am so scared I cannot move!
I'm frozen here with dread!
I saw a gruesome monster
hiding right beneath my bed!
I can't describe him to you
'cause he's kind of hard to see.
I only caught a glance of him
when I got up to pee.
I see his long gray nose there
sticking out from underneath.
I know he has a hundred eyes
and fifty pointed teeth!
I know he has two ugly heads
and great big swiping claws!
I'm sure he likes to gobble
little kids up in his jaws!
I'll bet his breath and scaly feet
are slimy, cold, and smelly.
I know he thinks that soon
I'm going to wind up in his belly!
He thinks that I will leave this bed,
he thinks I'll take a chance!
But I will stay here even if
I have to wet my pants!
'Cause I can see his nose down there,
it's moldy, long, and gray...
So I will just keep sitting here
until he goes away!

FOOD FOR THOUGHT

Uncle Bill told me,
"You are what you eat."
I didn't believe him,
but now I'm a beet.

SHOW AND TELL

Today at school for Show-and-Tell
I brought my dinosaur.
I squeezed him through the windows.
(He was too big for the door.)

He gave a bow and danced a jig
and showed his teeth a-plenty,
and though he sneezed off Teacher's wig,
he did that accidentally.

At lunch he was the first in line
and ate up all the meat.
They had to order pizza
for the rest of us to eat.

At Recess me and all my friends
and Dino played outside.
He was too big for Hide-and-Seek
but perfect for a slide.

Back in class he helped me
with my science presentation.
I talked about extinction
and he was my demonstration.

In art we made a masterpiece,
and Teach was so impressed,
she didn't even mind too much
when Dino crushed her desk.

We all went to the playground
after school for basketball.
My dinosaur scored every point
because he was so tall.

We got ice cream to celebrate
but didn't have to pay,
'cause when the cashier saw him
she screamed and ran away.

I had a blast with Dino
both at school and at the park.
I think next week for Show-and-Tell
I'll bring my Great White Shark!

The Ball

We're all so excited, we just heard the news!
There's a big ball that's coming to town.
So pick out your necklace, your earrings and shoes,
and purchase a lovely ball gown.

Yes, the big ball is coming, and we cannot wait
till the day it's supposed to roll round.
So put on your lipstick and go find a date
for the big ball that's coming to town!

WASHING MACHINE

I think it was foolish and somewhat extreme to take my bath inside our washing machine!

SHARING

Tom gave Jean a tangerine,
so Jean gave him a plum.
Sam gave Joan a saxophone,
so she gave him a drum.
Kim gave Ben a colored pen,
so he gave her the glue…
And I gave Chris a single kiss,
and he gave me the flu!

CLIFFHANGER

We're stuck at the top of this cliff.
We really don't know where we're at.
We cannot climb down
or we'll fall to the ground
and we'll land with a terrible splat.

We were hiking about in the woods.
Then we wandered out here to this ledge.
Now we cannot go back
'cause we can't find the track,
so we're sitting up here on the edge.

There isn't too much we can do.
Either way that we go we are dead.
'Cause the woods are too deep
and the cliff is too steep
so we'll just have to wait here instead.

If you're looking to find us just go
to the valley and then in a jiff,
you will see us up here
in the air bright and clear
just a-chillin' on top of this cliff.

Yes, it's lovely out here on the ledge.
We're not scared and we'll never complain.
But if you have time
then we sure wouldn't mind
if you'd come pick us up in a plane!

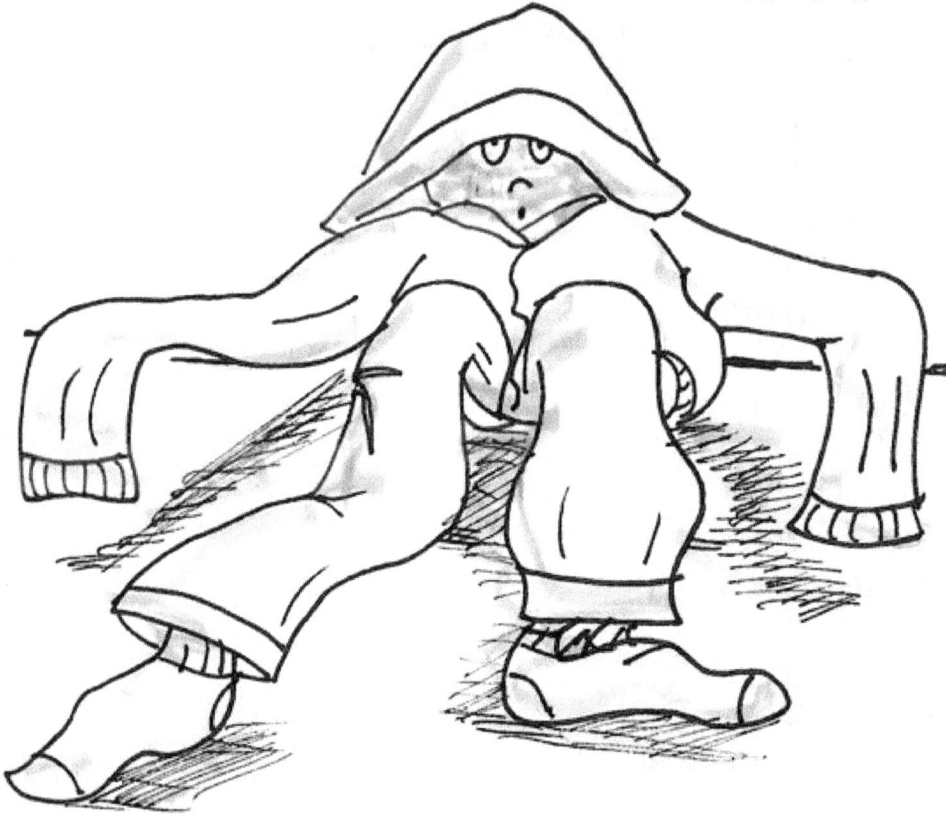

FITTING

These clothes just don't fit me,
don't fit me at all.
The socks are too big
and the pants are too tall.
These gloves are too large,
and this shirt is too wide.
This jacket could fit
two more people inside.
This scarf is enormous
and so is this sweater.
Dad's clothes just don't fit. . .
maybe Mom's will fit better.

FROZEN FACE

My mother always warned me
it's important that I never
make a face, because it just might
freeze that way forever.

But then one day when Tom called me
a jerk so impolitely,
I could not help but cross my eyes
and stick my tongue out slightly.

And then I found my eyes were stuck
still looking at my nose,
and drool from my protruding tongue
was clinging to my clothes.

No matter how I tried to move
the muscles in my face,
I simply, sadly could not shift
my features back in place.

And now it's been a year or more,
and I'm still stuck this way!
All 'cause I didn't listen
to what Mother had to say.

SAND CASTLE CONTEST

Look at this beautiful castle I made
out here on the sand with my bucket and spade.
It's perfectly sculpted, as smooth as can be.
I made it so tall it comes up to my knee!
It has windows and bridges and even a moat.
It has towers and flags, and I don't mean to gloat
but this contest for sure I am going to win!
Now what did you say 'bout the tide coming in?

STICKY FEET

I hate my stupid brother!
He filled my skates with glue.
And now I cannot get them off
no matter what I do.

And when I tried to be on time
for homeroom yesterday,
I rolled right by the classroom
and ran over Mrs. May.

Now bathing is impossible,
and sleeping is a pain.
Like last night when I sleepwalked
and woke up on Cherry Lane.

But there is still an up-side
to this life that's so bizarre. . .
You can bet your bottom dollar
I will never need a car!

SWING

I dared you to swing yourself over the bar…
I think that you took it a little too far!

ROMANTIC PLANTS

Some girls, they get tulips or roses.
My boyfriend is not good with plants.
He bought me a small Venus fly trap,
to pin to my dress at the dance.

Now the plant hasn't shut up all evening,
complaining with ravings and rants:
"The music is bad! There's no flies to be had!
We should go while we still have a chance!"
Oh, sometimes I think that my boyfriend
could brush up a bit on romance!

MAGIC BOOKMARK

In a box I found a bookmark
I had never seen before.
It looked like it had been there
for a hundred years or more.
My book was on the table,
so I stuck the bookmark in it—
and suddenly like magic, creatures
came out from within it!
A pirate, knight, and fairy,
and a beautiful princess
climbed right out of the pages,
and they made an awful mess!
The fairy wrecked our pantry
as she searched for bread and honey.
The pirate broke our china
and demanded all our money.
He turned and grabbed the princess
by the sleeve of her long gown.
She screamed so loud the neighbors shouted,
"Hey there, keep it down!"
The pirate moved back slowly
with the princess and his knife.
He said he wanted gold, or else
he'd take the maiden's life.
I tried to reach my bookmark
but he growled, "Just try and get it!"
The knight said, "Fiend! You hurt them
and I swear you will regret it!"
The villain roared with laughter
and it sent chills down my back.
The brave knight rushed right at him
with his sword raised to attack!
They clanged and banged and smashed stuff

till they tore the room apart.
The pirate pinned the knight down
with a dagger at his heart.
The princess started screaming
and she begged for his release.
Our neighbors hollered, "One more sound,
and we'll call the police!"
Just then the fairy flew in
with her honey and her bread.
She poured the honey jar out
on the wicked pirate's head.
The golden syrup blinded him.
It made him stop and stagger.
The knight knocked him unconscious
with the blunt hilt of his dagger.
"He got his gold!" the knight said
with a smile on his face.
The princess ran and kissed him
in a fairy tale embrace.
I saw I had my chance before
the whole thing got more weird.
I pulled the bookmark out quick
and they all just disappeared.
And now you're here and blaming me
that everything's all broken?
You think that I am lying,
and you say I must be jokin'?
I told you, Mom—it was the knight
and maiden in her dress!
This bookmark made them come alive
and caused this whole darn mess!
Well fine, then I will prove it
if you think the bookmark's fake!
I'll stick it here in... *Dracula!*
Ahh! Quick Mom, get a stake!

SORE THROAT

I'm Ralph McFords, I swallow swords,
I swallow them all day long—
and usually they go right down,
but this time something's wrong!

NUTS

A bag of mixed nuts
is full of a bunch
of different nuts
we like to munch.
Pecans and cashews,
peanuts and chestnuts.
They all are the same.
There are no "best nuts."

They don't care who's salty.
They don't care who's sweet.
'Cause every nut dances
to a different beat.
Nobody's judged
because of their face.
No one's excluded
because of their taste.

They all get along - no ifs, ands or buts.
So why can't people act like nuts?

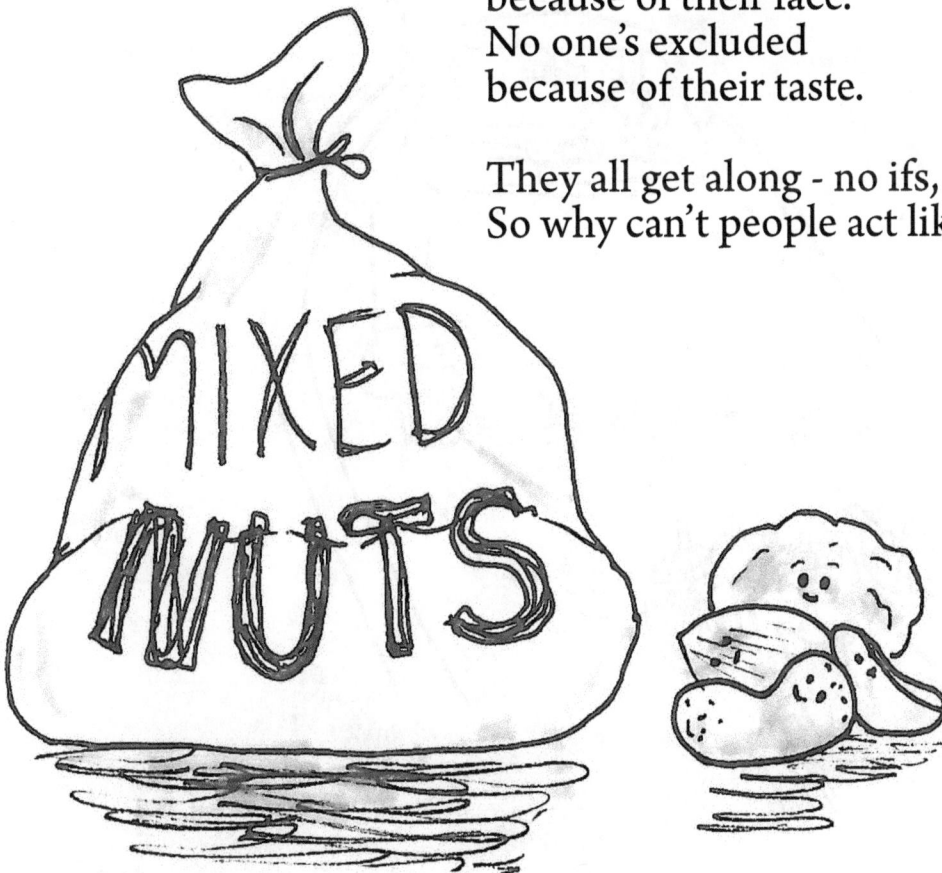

SPEEDING

I've been driving my car for ten years and three months.
I never have sped in it—not even once!
I don't run red lights or go over the limit,
but just now I noticed that for one full minute,
I've been closely followed by this angry cop!
His siren is on, and he's shouting, "Hey, stop!"
Now surely he'll say that I sped the whole time!
And what can I do? It's his word against mine.
So he'll give me a ticket as sure as can be. . . .
How come awful things only happen to me?

THE WORLD'S WORST DRINK

First we'll add some ginger ale
and some sludgy milk gone stale,
liquid soap and hardened custard,
thirteen eggs and spicy mustard,
soda, ketchup, salt and jam.
How 'bout paint? I'll add a can.
Then carrot juice, a hint of lime,
and grease and wax and turpentine.
What else should go into our drink?
Here's some bleach, shampoo, and ink,
and finally some lemonade—
and now at last our drink is made.
But first we'll add a cup of mud
and thirteen drops of human blood.

Now it's finished! Smells okay...
One cup each then we can say
we drank the world's most awful drink
right here out of our kitchen sink.
Here's your glass. Just let me fill it. . .
Now, be careful not to spill it.
Well? Why are you hesitating?
Drink it fast 'cause I am waiting
for you to go so I can follow.
Come on now just take one swallow!
The first sip always is the worst. . .
Hey, when did I say I'd go first?

THE BIRD IN THE CAGE

The bird in the cage knows nothing
of the world that lies beyond.
He's never fled from cats or fed
on breadcrumbs in a pond.

He's never built a nest or flown
into the setting sun.
He's never caught an earthworm
or escaped a hunter's gun.

He's never taken birdseed
from a lady's wrinkled hand.
He's never crossed an ocean
and just made it to the sand.

He's never lived high in a tree
or seen a foreign shore.
The only things he knows and trusts
are things he's seen before.

I often look around this world
and see how it's divided
between the birds that leave their cage
and those that stay inside it.

SLED DARE

Who out there will dare to ride
their sled down deadly Speedwell Street?
I've heard at least four kids have died
attempting to achieve this feat.
'Cause if you make it down the hill,
which is both steep and long you still
must then survive one final thrill:
A jump of fifty feet!

So if you dare to face this fright
come take the Sled-Ride Plunge of Doom.
Just close your eyes and hold on tight
and pray it will be over soon.
Come on now, are you prepared
to sled the hill, or are you scared?
Do you dare to try it out?

(I dared!)

LYING LAURA

"There's a tiger in my locker," Laura said to Miss McFinn.
"I cannot get my homework out 'cause he will do me in.
I can't retrieve my books or he will eat me, so I guess
I'll have to go and play instead of finishing my test."

But Miss McFinn said, "Laura, you are always telling lies,
and to believe you this time, I am sure, would not be wise.
You tell so many stories and they all are so absurd
that I would be a fool if I believed a single word.

Last week you said you couldn't take your social studies test
because you said your lungs were decomposing in your chest.
Two weeks ago, when you were seven hours late for school,
you said you'd fought a giant squid that you'd found in the pool.

From all your stories it would seem your dad's had five careers.
Your dog, you claim, has died eight times in just a couple years.
You've missed class twice and said you were out helping cops solve crimes.
You've fought space aliens and been abducted twenty times!

I'm sick of all this lying, Laura—I have had enough!
There's no tiger in your locker! I am going to call your bluff!
 I'm going to your locker now, and I will take a peek."

She strode into the hallway, we heard Laura's locker squeak.
Then came a lot of roaring and some screaming from the hall. . .
It seems that Lying Laura wasn't lying after all!

MY RESTAURANT

Welcome to my restaurant.
Please order anything you want!
Our specialty today is mud,
a glass of grass, or cup of crud
with sprinkled ants to chew and savor—
chopped-up worms will add some flavor.
Water? Guzzle from the hose
or puddles—we have lots of those.
At five o'clock you'll see a show.
We'll sit and watch the flowers grow.
And for dessert please have a slice
of woodchip cake with gravel spice!
So please relax and eat your fill,
but don't forget to pay the bill.
Hey wait, come back! Oh, what a jip!
No one ever leaves a tip!

TATTOO

I thought that Mom said I could get a tattoo,
so I went out and got one at noon.
She actually said I could get a tutu,
so now I am grounded till June.

JUGGLIN' JOE

Jugglin' Joe put on a show
at Orange County fair.
He grabbed a dozen apples
and he tossed them in the air.
And then he kept on jugglin'
whatever he could touch.
He added everything he saw
'cause nothing was too much:

He juggled a pie
and some marmalade cakes.
He juggled some jam
and some Salisbury steaks.
He juggled a hat
and a pair of red shoes.
He juggled eight staplers
and seventeen screws.
He juggled five turkeys
and one old spare tire.
He juggled ten torches
and lit 'em on fire.
He juggled twelve bowls
full of steaming clam chowder.
The crowd screamed for more
and grew louder and louder.

But I was up front,
and I wasn't impressed,
so I yawned really loud
once or twice I confess.
This was a mistake—
yes, indeed, 'cause you see,
that's when Jugglin' Joe
started jugglin' me!

PARTY OF ONE

She wanted to have a big party.
She set up the music and punch.
She took time to bake
a chocolate fudge cake,
and bought popcorn and pretzels to munch.

She cleaned and she hung decorations.
She showered and got nicely dressed.
She was ready by nine—
guess it just slipped her mind
that she never invited the guests!

HIRING POLICY

I only just got hired today
and I've been asked to go.
Exactly why I'm fired this way?
Well, that I just don't know!

I'm sure I did my job just fine,
and not one thing went wrong!
I brought the folks their food on time
and sang their birthday song!

I always washed my hands, I'm sure.
I was polite and nice. . .
I think it's just the manager
is not too fond of mice!

BOBBY IS AN ALIEN

Bobby is an alien.
I'm telling you it's true.
I sit behind him every day.
I've seen what he can do.
He's got a pocket radio,
I'm sure to contact Mars.
He's always sighing wistfully
and gazing at the stars.
He knows the weirdest facts and things
no normal kid should know.
Like what twelve times eleven is,
and what makes rockets go.
He speaks the strangest language.
 It's called something like "Ink lish."
And you should see the food he eats—
like chicken, beef, and fish.
His clothes are strange, his looks are strange.
Oh, teacher, hear me out!
Yes, Bobby is an alien,
of that there is no doubt.
Yes, Bobby is an alien,
but still I guess it's cool
to have a real live alien
at Planet Neptune School!

FISHING

I'm sick with flu and Mom's told me
I have to stay in bed.
She says she called the doctor and
that's what the doctor said.
But I've grown tired of lying here
with just one book to read.
I know! I'll use my fishing rod
to fetch the things I need:

Zip! I'll hook my comic books
with this ol' fishing line.
Zip! I'll hook the kitchen clock,
so I can check the time.
Zip! I'll hook my train set,
and I'll also hook the track.
Zip! I'll hook some cookies
just in case I want a snack.
Zip! I'll hook the TV set,
so I can watch my shows.
Zip! I'll hook my blanket
'case I want to warm my toes.
Zip! I'll hook the window shade
in case the sun's too bright.
Zip! I'll hook the table lamp
in case I need more light.
Zip! I'll hook the ceiling fan,
so I can have a breeze.
Zip! I'll hook my stereo
and all of my CDs.
Zip! I'll hook some toys and games
in case I want to play.
Zip! I'll hook the trash can
just to throw some stuff away.

Zip! I'll hook my hamster and
I'll also hook the cat.
Zip! I'll hook my cell phone,
so my friends and I can chat.

Hooray! I just got all I need
and never left my covers.
Now I can play the whole day long
and still obey my mother.
My fishing rod's the perfect plan—
there's nothing that can spoil it!
As long as I can figure out
a way to hook the toilet!

HOW TO USE UP ALL YOUR WHITEOUT

Using all your Whiteout is more simple than you think:

· Draw a picture of your teacher. Make sure that you use ink.
· Give her pimples and bucked teeth and bulging froggy eyes.
· Make her fat with stink lines and attracting many flies.
· Add lots of yucky details. (Like scales on her rear.)
· Write naughty words all over it. Make sure her name is clear!
  Then once your drawing's finished and you're sure you did your best...
· Turn it over just to find the front's your English test!

OBNOXIOUS

I wrote this poem but must admit
you won't get much from reading it.

Told ya!

THE BEAVER SONG

I'm a Beaver!
You're a Beaver!
We are Beavers all!
And when we get together,
we do the Beaver Call!
Neener neener neener! Neener neener nee!
Neener neener neener! Neener neener nee!

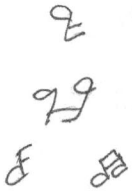

Beavers like to leap!
Beavers like to prance!
So when we get together
we do the Beaver Dance!
Neener neener neener! Neener neener nee!
Neener neener neener! Neener neener nee!

Beavers like to build!
Beavers like to plan!
So when we get together
we build a Beaver Dam!
Neener neener neener! Neener neener nee!
Neener neener neener! Neener neener nee!

Beavers love their music!
Beavers love their rap!
So when we get together
we do the Beaver Clap!
Clap clap clap clap clap clap! Clap clap clap clap clap!
Clap clap clap clap clap clap! Clap clap clap clap clap!

Beavers like to sing!
They sing the whole day long!
So when we get together
we sing the Beaver Song!
Neener neener neener! Neener neener nee!
Neener neener neener! Neener neener nee!

HALLOWEEN SPIRIT

It's Halloween night and we want a good fright,
so let's go to the castle that's up on the hill!
They say that it's haunted, but we won't be daunted
in finding our Halloween holiday thrill.
We'll climb the front porch, and we'll light up a torch,
and the doorbell will summon a chorus of bats.
The hallways will creak, and we may hear a squeak,
'cause I've heard that the floorboards are crawling with rats.
In the basement we'll find awful beasts of some kind,
and the portraits will follow us with moving eyes.
Outside in the gloom, we'll find Dracula's tomb—
and if we are lucky, we may see him rise.

There'll be blood in the faucets and skulls in the closets,
a kitchen with potions piled high on a shelf,
and ghouls in the bedrooms with festering head wounds
will sing to an organ that plays by itself.
In the turret up top we will make our last stop,
where we'll hear spirits sigh and the grim witch's groans.
If we look in the corner, I really should warn ya—
I'm sure we'll see piles of fresh rotting bones.

Then the lightning will flash and the thunder will crash,
and the old pirate zombie will rattle his chains,
as we dine with the ghosts and eat maggoty toast
that is smothered in toenails and mashed-up raw brains.
Yes, I have it all planned for a Halloween grand,
our nightmarish fun with the unruly dead. . .
though it is getting late, and remember by eight
we all gotta' be home in bed!

ENTER

Enter a garden of magic,
of epic adventures and thrills,
of milky white flowers
and silver rain showers,
and fields full of bright daffodils.

Enter a forest of mystery
where elves leap and dart through the trees,
where the air smells of pine,
and the silver streams shine,
and fairy nymphs dance in the breeze.

Enter a palace of music,
of stories that never were told,
where unicorns hide
in the bushes outside,
and the sun splashes fountains of gold.

Any person may enter these places.
You'll never need doorways or keys.
All you need is creation
and imagination
to take you wherever you please.

FISH FOOD

Last night I thought I'd fry some fish.
I cooked it in a silver dish.
And oh, how good my meal was smelling,
till my goldfish started yelling:

"Hey, how'd you like it if I took
your friend off a fishing hook
and peeled his skin off, fried him up,
and ate him for my Monday sup?
I'm your goldfish, don't you see?
To eat fish is like eating me!
Now please treat that poor fish you've fried
the way you'd treat me if I died!"

I felt so bad, I must confess,
that he was right to show distress.
I took the cooked fish off my plate
and buried it out by the gate.
Came back in, and then I thought
I'd eat another thing I bought.
And so, not to be thought a savage,
I decided to boil cabbage.
But just as I had got it steaming,
my new houseplant started screaming!

HELP

I pulled on my sweatshirt
but something went wrong
and my head just went somewhere
my arm should belong.

Now I can't move or see
though I'm struggling to try
so I'll just have to sit here
till someone comes by.

THE GIANT WORM BEAST

For two whole long years and a day and a half
I have searched for the giant worm beast.
And if you had asked me if I feared his wrath,
I'd have told you, "No, not in the least."
The knight called him frightening, and so did the knave,
but unlike those cowards I'm daring and brave,
and I've tracked him right down to his hot, windy cave—
this supposedly Giant Worm Beast.

I have climbed the high mountains and crossed all terrain
to search for the Giant Worm Beast.
And straight up to now my whole search was in vain,
though despite that I have never ceased.
The rumors all said he was fifty feet long,
with teeth sharp as razors and jaws quick and strong.
I guess I have proved that the rumors are wrong,
for I've captured the Giant Worm Beast!

WORLD'S BIGGEST SANDWICH

The biggest sandwich ever made
was built by my friend Paul.
A hundred fifty pounds it weighed
and measured ten feet tall.

It had six layers of turkey
and some pickles piled inside,
some bacon and beef jerky,
and a pound of chicken fried.

He added roast potatoes
with some ham and shredded beef,
some lettuce and tomatoes
with hot peppers underneath.

On thick white bread with Swiss cheese
he spread hot sauce—just a drop,
and sprinkled it with chickpeas
and an olive on the top.

A dash of pepper and at last
Paul's sandwich was completed.
Now all he has to do is
figure out a way to eat it!

HAIR CUT

Sarah McNair has such lovely long hair,
it hangs all the way to her knees.
Each time she is out she will shake it about,
so it flies just like silk in the breeze.
And when she's inside she will flip it with pride,
yes, she'll toss it whenever she can. . .
But today it was hot, and I guess she forgot
she was sitting so close to the fan!

FRED

Did you hear 'bout little Fred
who one day wouldn't leave his bed?
I'm not sure why, I just suppose he
thought that it was just too cozy.

Though his mother coaxed and pleaded,
nothing that she did succeeded.
She offered him ice cream and fudge
but Freddy still refused to budge.

She offered him some toys instead
but Fred just smiled and shook his head
and snuggled deep beneath the sheets,
refusing all the toys and treats.

He loved the way the blankets felt.
He loved the way the pillow smelt.
He worked himself into a groove,
and then he just refused to move.

His mother finally gave up trying,
stopped her coaxing, begging, crying.
Started bringing all Fred's meals
on those little carts with wheels.

She bought a fan to keep him cool.
She brought all of his books from school.
His friends came by 'bout once a week.
(Don't ask me how he took a leak.)

And on the day that he was wed,
he still refused to leave that bed.

But, my friends, I can assure you,
Freddy's life is not good for you.

Now he's dozing way up high.
His blanket is the starry sky.
The cloud's his pillow, soft and white.
The silver moon is his nightlight.

I promise that this story's true,
and so it could happen to you!
So learn a lesson from poor Fred,
and never buy a comfy bed!

THE OCEAN IS PURPLE

The ocean is purple.
The sky is dark green.
The trees are both lavender and tangerine.
The sand's just been finished and couldn't be redder.
The real world is boring—
My painting is better!

CAMP SCREAM-A-LOT

I'm going to Camp Scream-A-Lot
way out by Terror Lake.
That's where my folks are sending me
to spend my summer break.

I'll be up in the Haunted Cliffs
right off of Horror Coast.
I've heard those woods have werewolves
and our cabin has a ghost.

The sinks are full of spiders
and the toilets crawl with snakes.
Supposedly a crocodile
is living in the lake.

The dining hall I hear, is prone
to frequent bear attacks.
The counselors are cannibals
who eat the kids for snacks.

I'm going to Camp Scream-A-Lot.
It doesn't sound too cool. . .
Is it too late to fail a class
and go to Summer School?

Excuse

You want to know why I was late
for English class today?
And if I don't have an excuse
there's trouble on the way?

I do have an excuse,
and it's a very good one too.
So if you'll kindly take a seat,
I'll tell it all to you.

Comfy now? Alrighty then.
Allow me to begin…
The whole thing started when—
oh dear, there's something on your chin.

What? Why are you glaring?
I just had to point it out!
You can't have something on your chin
while walking all about!

All right! OK! I'll tell you now
about my great excuse—
if you'll just wait a minute
'cause I have to tie my shoes.

Why are you getting angry?
I am going to tell it all.
But this is more important.
I don't want to trip and fall!

There! All tied and pretty!
Now I'll tell it all to you.
Except that I've just noticed
that the blackboard's dirty too!

It's really very filthy, ma'am.
The worst I've ever seen!
Let me get some soap suds—there!
Now it's all nice and clean.

Okay! I'll tell my story.
I will give it one more try.
See, here's why I was late today—
Whoops! There's the bell! Goodbye!

MY HAMSTER'S ADDICTED TO CHOCOLATE!

My hamster's addicted to chocolate.
My gerbil eats cookies and cakes.
My little gray rabbit cannot kick his habit
of sipping on strawberry shakes.

My puppy loves double-cheese pizza.
My cat likes fried chicken for lunch.
My fish cannot budge 'cause he's swimming in fudge
and my snake just eats Cinnamon Crunch.

My animals eat too much junk food.
So now I am calling their vets.
And I'm starting to see why my parents told me
I shouldn't share food with my pets!

ODE TO A COMPUTER

I hate this dumb computer.
It does not work for me.
It will not download anything.
It won't type properly.
The graphics aren't super.
It's slow, there is no doubt.
And every time I turn it on,
the house lights all go out.
So now I've come up with a plan:
I'll take my baseball bat!
You stupid old computer,
take this and that and that!
I've fixed my dumb computer.
It should give me no more trouble,
'cause it has been upgraded to
a smoking pile of rubble!

COASTIN'

We're all aboard the fastest
roller coaster in the world.
In just a couple minutes
we'll go shooting towards the ground
from seven hundred feet
where we'll be swung and flung and hurled
through thirty loops at ninety miles
an hour round and round.

Yes, this is Killer Coaster—
It's the world's most scary ride,
and few of those who've ridden it
have lived to tell the tale.
It's said that flames will shoot at us
from every single side,
and someone told me yesterday
its brakes are known to fail.

There aren't any seatbelts,
you'll be clinging by your fists,
and sometimes all the cars are known
to tumble off the track.
So make sure you are holding tight
for all the turns and twists,
'cause there is quite a likely chance
we won't be coming back.

Now we have reached the top where we
will shoot off like a jet. . .
We're going down. . .we're soaring. . .
and we're back, fit as a fiddle!
Well, I thought it was fun.
I don't know why you're so upset!
Okay, I guess I may have tried
to scare you just a little. . .

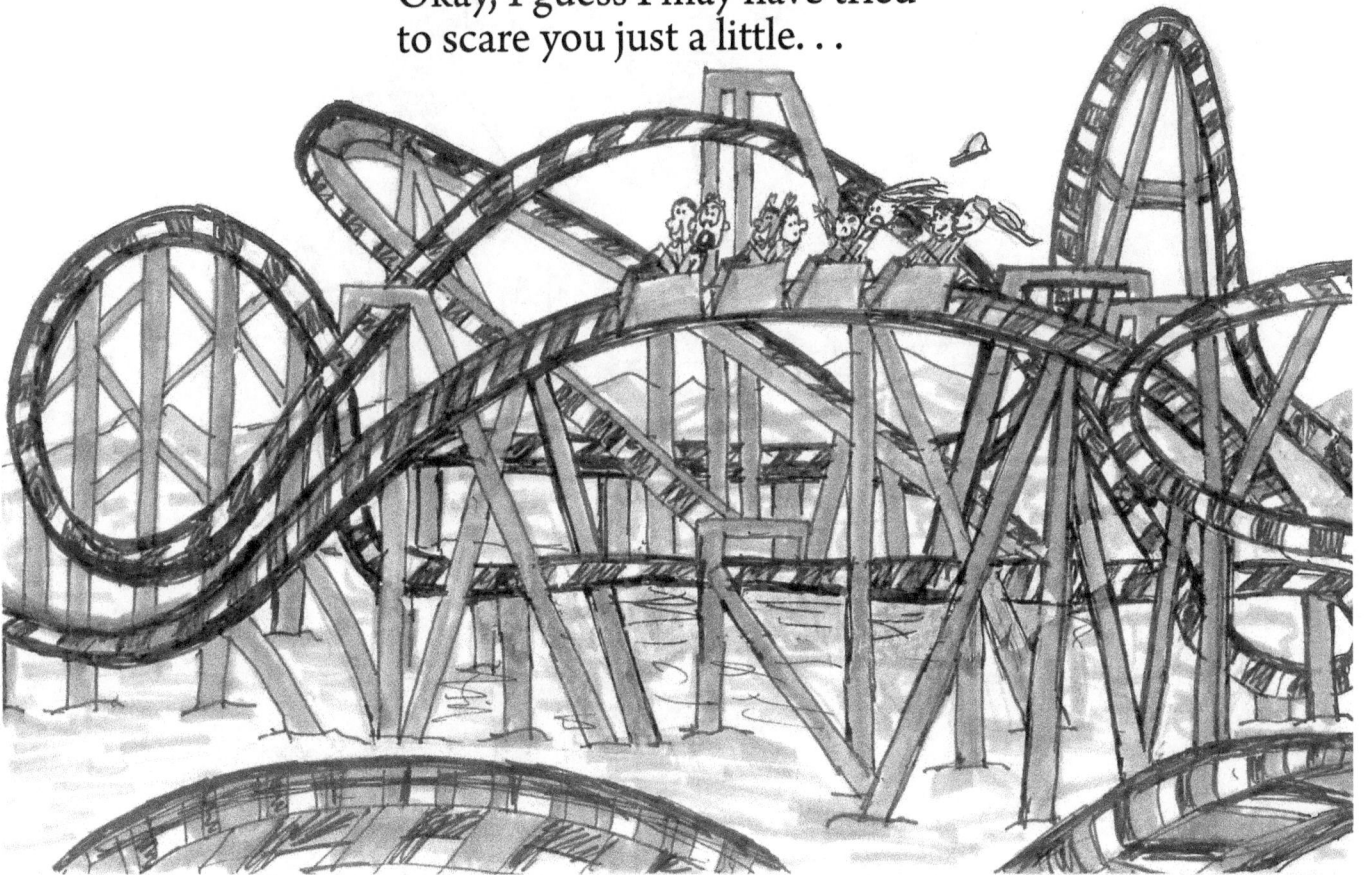

KATE'S DESK

Kate's desk is the messiest I've ever seen!
Inside there's a sandwich all moldy and green.
Her markers are dried up, her papers are crinkled,
her smelly used gym socks are crusty and wrinkled.
She's chewed up her pencils and left all the tips
between wads of gum and some bent paper clips.
Kate's desk is disgusting—but here is the shocker:
You think this is bad? Have a look in her locker!

THE CONTINUED STORY OF THE THREE LITTLE PIGS

Remember the story "The Three Little Pigs"
from when you were a kid?
About a wolf that tried to catch three pigs
and never did?

The story ends when our wolfy friend
falls into the fireplace.
He lands in a pot that's boiling hot
and leaves without a trace.

Is the story done? Have the piggies won?
Most readers tend to bet
that the wolf will return, in spite of his burn
'cause the fight's not over yet.

Way down south by the river mouth
is where three houses are.
One made of bricks, the second sticks.
The third is built of straw.

A wolf walked by beneath the sky.
The sun spilled pools of gold.
And though its light was warm and bright
the wolf felt bitter cold.

He'd felt this way ever since the day
he failed to catch three pigs.
The homes of his foes had looked like those. . .
of straw and bricks and twigs.

The wolf stopped dead. He raised his head
and gave a little shiver.
"Those are the dwellings!" he burst out yelling,
"Down there by the river!"

The wolf smiled slightly, his teeth gleamed brightly.
He thought of his defeat.
"Today's the day those pigs will pay!
Revenge will be so sweet!"

The first house he saw was made of straw.
He'd blown it down before.
"Those pigs never learned," said the wolf as he burned
the straw house to the floor.

The pig burst out with a terrified shout
when he saw that his house was ablaze.
And the wolf standing there gave a terrible stare
that met the pig's horrified gaze.

Thus started the chase to the second pig's place,
where the first pig slipped inside.
"That is hardly the sort," said the wolf with a snort,
"of place where I would hide."

The wolf looked around till he saw on the ground
some bugs, which he placed on the wood.
These termites had cravings and left only shavings
where once the house had stood.

The pigs ran away from the pile of decay
to the third pig's house—the last.
"That brick house was tough," thought the wolf in a huff,
so he thought up another plan fast.

He went to the store, then came back up the shore
as the pigs all watched in fright.
He put in the sand what he'd had in his hand:
three sticks of dynamite!

"Quick, follow me!" whispered pig number three,
and led his two friends out the back.
While the wolf lit each stick and threw them in quick,
the piggies hid from his attack.

Concealed in the bushes, they sat on their tushes,
then came a big KABOOM!
There was fire and smoke, and it made them all choke
and the day grew as black as a tomb.

When at last the dust cleared the three piggies cheered.
They thought that the wolf must be dead.
"He could never have done the deed and still run
away in time!" they said.

So the pigs danced around on the black and burned ground,
and none of them happened to see
the wolf as he stepped from the stream where he'd leapt,
and came toward the piggies with glee.

Is the story done? Have the piggies won?
I'll give you just one clue:
There was quite a slaughter that day by the water. . .
then the wolf had a barbeque.

MAGICAL MAX AND ME

Magical Max is renowned for his acts.
He's the town's most impressive magician.
At quarter past six every day he does tricks,
charging just a few dollars admission.
He'll make cars disappear, pull a coin from your ear,
'cause he's always on top of his game.
I've heard from a few of my friends he can do
just about any trick you can name.
But I don't understand what's so great or so grand
about Magical Max, for you see,
I do magic tricks too - every day, yes it's true,
and I'm much more impressive than he.
Although I'm not able to vanish a table
or even a very small ball.
There's one trick I know that I do every show,
and Max never does it at all.
This trick is so great! I just stand here and wait
till the people in front start to yawn.
And each time I've found when I turned back around
all the folks who were watching are gone.
Yes, Magical Max and his magical acts
all come second to me, it is clear.
For in all the land only I alone can
make my whole audience disappear!

BOOMERANG

Today I bought a boomerang.
But I am such a jerk—
I threw it and it won't come back.
I guess it doesn't work.

BAD DAY

Today has been an awful day,
the worst I've ever known.
I shouldn't have gone out at all.
I should have stayed at home.

I overslept and missed my bus.
It left just as I came.
I had to walk to school instead
in freezing, pouring rain.

I tried to take a shortcut,
but I got stuck in a bog.
I lost my shoes in mud and
I got chased by someone's dog.

And when I finally got to school
all cut up, bruised and scraped,
my teacher marked me tardy
'cause she said that I was late.

She asked me for my homework,
and I guess I should have known,
that like a fool I'd left it
sitting on my desk at home.

So teacher made me go and share
a book with Robbie Rhine,
whose nose is always running
and who smells bad all the time.

When lunchtime came I found out that
my backpack had a rip.
My lunch sack must have fallen out
along my morning trip.

And once back in the classroom,
Teacher sprang a Spanish test.
I'm pretty sure I failed it
even though I tried my best.

And if that wasn't bad enough,
just to be extra cruel,
she gave me lots of homework
and she kept me after school.

For dinner Mom made broccoli
and icky lima beans,
and then I spilled tomato sauce
right down my favorite jeans.

Today has been an awful day,
so terrible and long,
and everything I've tried to do
has somehow turned out wrong.

But I will keep on smiling,
I won't go to bed in sorrow.
'Cause I know that a bad day means
a better day tomorrow!

I'll Never Kiss A Girl

I'll never kiss a girl, oh no,
I'll never kiss a girl.
It's just about the most disgusting
notion in the world.
I'd kiss a crocodile,
a giant cockroach or a squirrel.
I'd do a lot of things,
but I would never kiss a girl.

I'll eat a plate of liver
and a bowl of brussel sprouts.
I'll dive into a shark tank
with no second thoughts or doubts.
I'll swing by just my ankles
from a mile-high trapeze.
I'll run right through a torrent
of some angry stinging bees.

But. . .

I'll never kiss a girl, oh no,
I'll never kiss a girl.
It's just about the most disgusting
notion in the world.
(But I admit that, sometimes
when I talk to Kelly Bearl,
perhaps on one occasion
I could maybe kiss a girl.)

BREEZY SKIING

You say you wish to learn to ski?
I have good news, my dear!
Like me, you can learn twice as quick
by getting special gear.

You can get a good strong helmet
that will keep your head protected.
A bright chord in an avalanche
will help you be detected.

Some thicker gloves and ski socks
keep your toes and fingers toastin'.
A trendy new snow jacket
makes you look good when you're coastin'.

You can buy some special goggles
so the snow won't make you blind,
and extra-padded ski pants
so you don't bruise your behind.

With all this stuff you'll look cool
and you'll learn to ski with ease—
(Unless you are like me and you
forget to buy the skis…)

THE WIZZLEWOP

Last night as I lay dreaming
in a sweet and peaceful doze,
a Wizzlewop snuck in my room
and nibbled off my toes.
And when I woke this morning
well, imagine all my shock,
when I got up to go to school
and found I couldn't walk!
But teacher, here's the worst part,
though I'm sure you'll understand
that since my toes are gone
and I can barely even stand,
I cannot walk or run or jump
in any kind of way.
So I guess I can't participate
in P. E. class today!

SIMPLE POWER

Who sees the world in a grain of sand
and heaven in a flower?
Those of us who understand
that simple things have power.

The tallest tree in all the wood
began the smallest seed.
The path of our whole future could
be changed by just one deed.

A single shot could start the war
a single smile could cease.
One friendship built could help secure
a path to future peace.

A wiser world would understand
that simple things have power.
And see the world in a grain of sand
and heaven in a flower.

LAST PAGE

This last page we left blank for you
to put in something of your own:
to stick a photo in with glue,
to draw a picture, write a poem,
to talk about a dream you had
or anything you do for fun…
Nothing that you want to add?
Then just stick in your chewing gum!

INDEX

ABOUT THE AUTHORS

Jennifer Sleeper (left) and Debbie Sleeper (right) are identical twins born in London, England. They grew up living in Europe and the United States and have been writing children's poems together since they were seven. Debbie and Jennifer base their poetry on their own experiences as kids: going to school, attending summer camp and having adventures with their friends and family. Both girls have also been drawing since a young age. They share a wacky sense of humor, which usually finds its way into their illustrations and cartoons.

Debbie and Jennifer both currently live in Orlando, Florida.

www.ingramcontent.com/pod-product-compliance
Lightning Source LLC
Chambersburg PA
CBHW081233090426
42738CB00016B/3285